D0955493

— DO —
YOU!

- DO -
YOU !

INSPIRATION & ENCOURAGEMENT
FOR ANYONE WHO WAS EVER
BULLIED, LEFT OUT,
OR PUSHED ASIDE

· BEN COHEN ·
Founder of the StandUp Foundation

▷|◁

PAM KRAUSS BOOKS
NEW YORK

Published in the United States by Pam Krauss Books,
an imprint of the Crown Publishing Group, a division of
Penguin Random House LLC, New York.

www.crownpublishing.com

PAM KRAUSS BOOKS and colophon are trademarks of Penguin
Random House LLC.

Library of Congress Cataloging-in-Publication Data

Cohen, Ben, 1978–
Do you : inspiration and encouragement for anyone who was ever
pushed aside, left out, or bullied / Ben Cohen. — First edition.
1. Bullying—Prevention—Juvenile literature. 2. Self-esteem—
Juvenile literature. 3. Conduct of life—Juvenile literature. I. Title.
BF637.B85C63 2015
302.34'3—dc23

2015000331

ISBN 978-0-8041-8564-6
eBook ISBN 978-0-8041-8565-3

Printed in the United States of America

Book and jacket design by Laura Palese

10 9 8 7 6 5 4 3 2 1

First Edition

TO
you

introduction

"Ignore it, and they'll eventually get bored and pick on someone else."

"You just need to develop a thicker skin." "Can't you take a joke?" "Come on, a little teasing won't kill you."

If you are the target of bullying, I bet you've heard something similar from certain people in your life. If you have felt hopeless and thought to yourself, *They just don't get it,* you're right, they don't. I know as well as anyone that bullying doesn't go away unless it is addressed and that yes, it can hurt—even kill.

True story: My dad was savagely beaten and killed by a gang of thugs when he stood up for an employee who was being bullied. Just for stepping in to protect someone who was being victimized. It made me realize that bullying goes far beyond the supposedly good-natured horseplay that happens in the locker room or casual name calling we all hear on street

And as I've learned, the best way to defeat the bullies is by doing what you do best—in fact better than anyone else on the whole planet—and that is DO YOU.

corners or in school hallways every day. Seeing my father die at the hands of others made me realize that bullying of *any* kind is unacceptable—there is no level at which it is okay. It's all on a spectrum of just plain wrong. And it made me want to do something about it.

When I retired from playing rugby professionally in 2011 (just after being named Player of the Year) to launch the StandUp Foundation, many people thought I was crazy. But I knew that as a professional athlete and World Cup champion, I had a voice, and I needed to use that voice to make a real difference in the world. I needed to help people like you, and a million other people you or I may know and the millions more we don't, stand up for themselves and take the power back from the bullies.

"Faggot ... loser ... beaver teeth ... lard ass ... retard."

These are just a few of the choice names I've heard of people being called in my travels around the world as an anti-bullying advocate. I've heard stories of kids getting stuffed into lockers and being hounded by online messages saying that they were too ugly to be seen in public. There are tales of beatings and bruises, both physical and psychological, which make me wonder how human beings—of all ages—can inflict such cruelty on one another.

Even if you're not being physically assaulted, bullying hurts. It's painful, isolating, and often very frightening. But you don't need me to tell you that. If you're reading this, chances are that you—or someone you love—are already familiar with the damage bullying causes. If you're living through it—or have lived it—please know that I feel your pain and I understand.

And as I've learned, the best way to defeat the bullies is by doing what you do best—in fact better than anyone else on the whole planet—and that is DO YOU.

Throughout this book, you will find suggestions to help you deal with the bullies in your life, to make a game plan, and to find the teammates and coaches who will help you put that game plan into action. You will also hear from some of the StandUp supporters and bullying survivors I've had the privilege of working with on this journey.

I hope *Do You* will provide both inspiration and practical advice to help you get through with your head held high and your heart and soul intact. In my case, as in the cases of so many others, these lessons were hard-earned. In the end, they are what turned me into a champion, not just in rugby, but in life. I wish the same for you. Let me hear from you, and know, always, that I am in your corner. #DoYou.

—Ben Cohen

1

the

secret

POWER

CALLED

"YOU"

Here's the truth about bullying: The bully's goal is to make you be someone or something other than yourself. He or she wants to make you give up and quit the thing you are the very best at: and that's being *you*.

And sometimes, we agree to it, especially when intimidation or violence is pointed our way. That kind of pressure clouds our thinking, making it easy to get confused about how somebody who doesn't even really know us can have so much influence over what we do, where we go, and how we act. But trying to change the way another person acts or feels or looks or anything else is just totally and completely and undeniably wrong.

So here's a bit of advice: When you are feeling bullied, intimated, scared, or confused—when you feel you don't know what to do—just do you.

Nobody knows you better than you do. You know what's right for you. You know where you are comfortable, real, and wonderful. When bullying causes you to question those things, you can choose to push back with the unbreakable power that is you. Nobody else has that power or will ever have it. Nobody else knows how to have it. Just you. It's your secret power.

IF THEY DO BAD,
DO YOU.

IF THEY DO UGLY,
DO YOU.

IF THEY DO NASTY,
DO YOU.

IF THEY DO MEAN,
DO YOU.

IF THEY DO WRONG,
DO YOU.

No matter what they do, you should do you.

You do you. Better than anyone ever has. So just keep on doing you, no matter what.

NO MATTER WHAT THEY DO, YOU SHOULD DO YOU.

#DOYOU

Let's just say it plainly: You matter more than bullies do. They want you to believe differently, but that is exactly what gives them power.

You matter more than the bullies. Period. And you have to believe that and live that.

But, easier said than done, right? After all, if standing up in the face of bullying was NBD, you probably wouldn't be reading this book. You'd be out there—anywhere and everywhere—just being you. Doing you sort of stuff. Instead, you've found this book to help you through some painful times.

So you're sitting in your room, reading this book. Probably not feeling so great right now. And this wasn't the plan. No way.

You actually have to *do* something to feel better. And you've already done something: You've chosen to read this book. It's your first step in your journey, but it's just a start. Why help the bullies in their mission to make you feel bad?

2
WHO
REALLY
matters?

DO YOU.

DON'T JUST

BE YOU.

#DOYOU

We can sit around and focus on how *wrong they are*. But why waste another minute thinking about them? Let's focus on you instead.

You, and what you do. And how right that is. And how interesting life will be when you do you.

When we get right down to it, standing up for yourself is hard work. And some days, it might seem too hard. That's okay. For a minute. Or a day. But not forever and not for most of the time. If doing you is feeling too hard, or too scary, or just too overwhelming, then we have work to do. Work called "you."

So let's get to what matters.

And what matters is you.

The world needs you. You are, after all, the only you that the world has. If *you* don't do you, then who will?

Do you.
Don't just be you.
Being is the start.
Doing is the art.

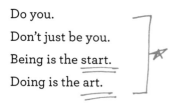

3

reject

THE

REJECTIONS

Bullying, rejection, intimidation, and humiliation. Not even fun words to read. Living through the reality of them has been more than some people could stand.

You've heard about them. Their stories are heartbreaking. Know this: We don't want you to become one of them. You don't, either. So let's not let it happen.

But we need to get really clear on this: You have to stand up. First, inside, to yourself. Then, outside, to others. You depend on it.

If all the energy and promise that is you is being mistreated, something needs to be done about that. Not tomorrow—right now.

One of the first steps in getting ready to do you is to insist upon yourself. Just the very act of you declaring you. Holler it out loud. And I mean *loud*.

One of the first steps in getting ready to do you is to insist upon yourself. Just the very act of you declaring you. Holler it out loud. And I mean *loud*.

I AM.

I AM HERE . . .

I AM HERE TO

DO ME!

I AM HERE TO DO ME

IN MY
OWN
WAY!

Anybody who tells you otherwise is trying to push a different idea of yourself on you.

To hush you up.

To make you not do you.

And that's not okay.

Bullies will try to convince you that it is *your* fault they pick on you, that the way you look or act or think or *whatever* is done just to provoke them, that if you could just be *normal* they wouldn't have to pick on you.

What? No way! That logic is twisted, and you can't buy into it. Being bullied is the fault of one person only, and that person is *not* you.

Who is that person or those people, anyway? What makes them think they know how you should do you better than you do? They don't—they only know how to do them.

The bullies want you to enter into an agreement with them. They want to have some kind of strange, unhealthy, hurtful relationship with you. One you do not want. One you do not deserve. One that says they are going to decide what's cool, what's "right," what's up, and that you aren't. Why do only they get to decide? They don't. Don't let them make you agree to something you know is wrong.

4

DON'T

SIGN

the
contract

Refuse the contract they want you to sign. You know the one. The one that says you will *be someone other than who you really are.*

If you've already signed that contract—already accepted or agreed to what other people want you to think about yourself—then break it. Tear it up. Throw it away. *No deal.*

You don't need a lawyer to void this particular contract. You don't even need to say a single word about it. Just do you. That will be a full, complete, and permanent shredding of the bullying contract.

When you do you, you are writing your own terms. You are drafting your *real deal* for life. It's a deal with yourself that says:

I have every right to be respected.

To be included.

To have friends.

To feel love.

To be goofy and weird and great and confused.

To be perfect in my imperfections.

Why? Because you're you.

No other reason needed.

Signed. Sealed. Delivered.

BULLYING IS NOT A RITE OF PASSAGE.
NO ONE EVER HAS TO "MAN UP."

—WALTER, WASHINGTON, D.C.

ONE OF THE WORST FORMS OF BULLYING
I HAVE ENCOUNTERED IS
SIMPLY BEING IGNORED . . . SITTING
BY MYSELF AT A LUNCH TABLE,
PEOPLE MOVING AWAY
FROM ME, PEOPLE NOT ACKNOWLEDGING
THAT I EVEN EXIST.

—DIANA, NEW YORK

. THE .
REAL DEAL,
NO-BULLY
CONTRACT

Write your own contract.

What are your terms for the kinds of friendships you are willing to have? What is allowed behavior from those in your life? To whom do you grant permission to be part of your life, and to whom do you say, "No deal"? Put it down in black and white, and make it the real deal.

DATE: _____   CONTRACT DRAFTED BY: _____

It is hereby written that I believe these behaviors and actions are good to be around:

_____
_____
_____
_____
_____
_____

And I will NOT tolerate the following behaviors and actions:

_____
_____
_____
_____
_____
_____

So, it is then resolved that I will no longer allow a relationship with:

_____
_____
_____
_____
_____
_____

SIGNED,

_____

YOU!

WITNESSED BY:

_____

(someone who loves you, btw)

5
channel

Getting things clear
in your own head is a pattern
you have to repeat. It's a signal
you have to find and stay with.

You may need to remind yourself of this every single
day—maybe even many times a day—until you are
really tuned in. After all this time you've spent trying to be someone else—listening to someone else's
voice—it may take a little practice to remember how
to do you without a second thought. Or, think of it as a
daily workout, just like for any sport or skill you want
to perfect. Endurance will matter. After all, you have
to do you every day for the rest of your life.

TUNE IN TO YOU

#DOYOU

No sugar-coating: Things won't always be easy. But hey, they're probably not easy now. This is why getting clear in your own head matters. You're going to need to stay clear when things get rough.

Tune out what you've been hearing in your own head—or what others have been putting in it. And turn up the truth of you.

You know with certainty that you aren't being seen accurately, heard clearly, treated fairly, or included openly. That hurts to say, but it's okay. You've already felt the hurt. Finally saying it yourself is one way of dealing with the truth. You deserve better, and you know it. So listen to your own soundtrack, not theirs.

Your clear thinking and tuned-in voice will be required. After all, if bullies walked away or shut up every time we asked them to—well, they wouldn't be bullies, would they?

Tune in to you.

Do you.

Now that things are clear, it's no time to be quiet.

If you are suffering from bullying, being left out, or getting pushed aside, it is not okay, and you need to say so. Share what you've been through and use your voice.

TELL YOUR STORY.

TO SOMEONE.
TO EVERYONE.
TO ANYONE.
TO YOUR FAMILY,
FRIENDS,
COUNSELORS,
COACHES,
TEACHERS.

IT WILL BE HARD.

6

USE

YOUR

voice

NEVER PUT UP WITH BULLYING
AND NEVER BE SILENT.
SPEAK UP. NO ONE SHOULD
EVER MAKE YOU FEEL LIKE
YOU ARE WORTHLESS.

—IGNACIA, CALIFORNIA

TELL EVERYBODY WHO
THE AGGRESSOR IS. *EVERYBODY.*
BUILD A NETWORK THAT
MAKES HIS OR HER BEHAVIOR
IMPOSSIBLE TO IGNORE.

—ELI, MICHIGAN

The bullies want you to believe that if you stand up for yourself, if you use your voice, if you do you, you are somehow doing something wrong—to *them*.

THEY ARE LYING.

The truth is, bullying depends on secrecy. It doesn't happen out in the open very often for a reason—because the bullies know it is wrong, and others will stop them. By using your voice, by calling a bully a bully, you shine a light into the dark corners where bullying lurks.

WHEN YOU USE YOUR VOICE
WHEN YOU GIVE AWAY THE SECRET
WHEN YOU DO YOU
THAT'S WHEN THE BULLYING GETS EXPOSED.

That clear voice in your head? The one that insists on you? That knows you matter? That won't agree to the bad deal? You have to use it. Practice saying it to yourself first. Say it until you can yell it with confidence and conviction. Get ready to *roar*.

7

IT'S, LIKE

Okay

You don't need permission to enjoy who you like, what you like, or how you like it.

Just like what you like. And like it the way *you* like it. It's the best way to show the bullies they aren't going to win. BTW: You can't change what you like and neither can the bullies, so go ahead and like it!

Sure, maybe some people won't like the same things you do. Or like that you like things they don't. Or like that you don't like the same things they do. So what? We all like what we like, and that should be enough. Right? Right.

This wide world of likes—and the choices that come with it—is actually a pretty good thing. It means there is a place for all of us to fit in somewhere. And this is a place where what we like is shared by others. It's a place where who we like and who we spend our time with is our business and no one else's. And where we might *not* fit is just as clear. After all, none of us fit in everywhere, so it is important to find the *right* fit for who we are.

When you do you, all the pieces around you just seem to fit better. The people around you like you for you. The patterns of life make a bit more sense. And you just feel more comfortable in your own skin. Or crazy clothes. Or favorite T-shirt. Or worn-out boots. Who wants to wear a scratchy sweater that doesn't fit, anyway?

Go ahead.

Get comfortable in you.

It's where you were born to fit.

Comfortable with yourself? Getting closer to it at least? It's fine if the answer is "not yet." After all, every one of us is a work in progress. And, as long as you don't give up on you, that progress will happen. Even on the days when it feels as if you're stuck. Just keep doing *you* and let the world catch up with you.

> I had a best friend in high school, and one night I finally told her I was gay. I was so afraid she would turn away from me. . . . We are still in touch forty years later.
> —PAUL, NEW JERSEY

LIKE WHAT YOU LIKE, DO WHAT YOU DO

List the things you like doing the most. Not just ideas of things or general categories, but the actual activities you do. Be really specific—the details will help you know where you are most comfortable and the types of people you will enjoy the most.

I would click "like" on:

1. _____

2. _____

3. _____

4. _____

5. _____

6. _____

7. _____

8. _____

9. _____

10. _____

As you get more comfortable

with yourself—the parts you think are awesome, and the parts you want to work on, too—be sure to make room for people who like the you that you're growing into. This is going to be your new team—the one that picks you every time and never leaves you sitting on the bench.

Remember, doing you, becoming the *real* you, doesn't happen all at once. It takes time. You take time. You are worth taking that time. But that doesn't mean you need to go it alone. Bullies like it when you feel isolated and alone and scared. That's their goal. But it takes more than one team to play a tournament.

If you can, find other people who are on the same kind of journey you are. Along the way, you will find people you connect with through shared

interests and

curiosities and

respect.

(And here's a secret: They don't have to be in your class or live on your street. You can find people like you anywhere and everywhere. You just have to look for them.)

This is when the fun starts.

8
TEAM
up

> Find someone who can truly mentor you. If you talk to someone and anything comes out of their mouth that makes you feel like you are the problem, leave and move on to the next person.
>
> —BOBBY, GEORGIA

Soon enough—maybe suddenly—you will realize you're not trying to fit on someone else's team anymore— a team that keeps rejecting you. Instead, you're part of one in which you fit. One made up of a bunch of different people, doing a bunch of different things, but all supporting one another and cheering one another's victories. *THAT'S A TEAM.*

Truth is, nothing works on any team if we try to take someone else's position, to imitate his or her talent, or to make his or her play. We can only play our own positions, develop our own talents, and make our own plays. Bullies want to kick you out of your place and deny your talent. They ruin teams.

So build one of your own. People will come looking for you and all that makes you the unique person you are.

When they do, let them find you—let them in. Form your own team. When you do, you'll find it's just about impossible to be rejected or feel left out. It might take time, the wait may be lonely, and it will probably feel frustrating. But you have to hang in there because you are worth the wait.

The people I would like to have on my team:

_____

_____

_____

_____

_____

The talents I have and the plays I will make:

_____

_____

_____

_____

_____

> Seek out a community that supports the activities or skills that really interest you. There is always some person or group waiting to embrace you. Find them; they are waiting for you.
> —STEPHANIE, NEW YORK

9

YOU ARE

NOT

too....

Where will you take you next?
How are you going to do you?

What will make it happen? When do you feel most capable and comfortable? These are real questions, and you have the answers. The answers help define the *who* of your you.

Here's where to start. Take note of this. It's maybe the most important thing in this book.

YOU ARE NOT

TOO FAT,

TOO UGLY,

TOO QUEER,

TOO WEIRD,

TOO DARK,

TOO LIGHT,

TOO QUIET,

TOO LOUD,

TOO SKINNY,

TOO WEAK,

Too anything

AND MOST OF ALL,

YOU

ARE

NOT

TOO

YOU.

In fact, the world needs *more* you, not less. And to get through life, you are going to need to be *all* the you that you can possibly be.

That's the truth. It's your truth, but it's also *the* truth. And, nobody can deny it.

> I once told a bully I felt sorry for her, because her life must be very empty if she needed to make someone else feel like crap to feel better about herself.
>
> —KARA, ARIZONA

THE WORLD
NEEDS

**MORE
YOU,**

NOT LESS.

Let's take this up a notch, okay?

Maybe it all feels too hard, or even impossible. That's just fine—if you are just fine with being pushed aside, left out, or bullied. Of course, you are not just fine with that.

Let's turn the tables, shift the view, change the focus, and see things clearly.

Remember this: Anyone who bullies another person has something really, really wrong in his or her life. That person is trying to get rid of his or her pain by passing it along to you. The people who are the meanest are usually the ones who have been hurt the most. This doesn't necessarily mean you have to feel sorry for them, but it's something you need to know and think about. They hurt because they've been hurt. It's what they know and what feels familiar to them. But it shouldn't ever, *ever* become familiar to you.

Bullies don't know the meaning of the phrase "do you." They might not even realize it, but by targeting you, they only prove they don't have anything in their own life to focus on.

This doesn't excuse their behavior for one minute, but when you know what's really going on, you have the advantage of perspective—one that they just don't have.

10

get

PERSPECTIVE

THEY HURT

| BECAUSE THEY'VE |

BEEN HURT

When you find yourself on the receiving end of a bully's attention, ask yourself, *Why is this happening?* instead of *Why is this happening to ME?*

Doing so will let you see the truth: It's happening because of something sad in the bully's life, not because of you. Change your perspective on the bully, and it will help change your perspective on you.

You've done nothing wrong; you've just been doing you. Bullies would like to make you question that choice, but that's not an option. You have to push forward—and let the bullies find their own way without you.

No matter how hard it may seem, keep your focus:

THE BEST WAY TO
PUSH BACK
IS TO MOVE FORWARD.
DESTINATION: you

> I don't listen to the negative
> things people say,
> as they are useless to me.
> —CARSON, VIRGINIA

11

BE
PERFECTLY
imperfect

The more you *do* you, the more you'll *be* you.

Just repeat this cycle, and it will grow stronger and stronger.

Do you do you do you do you do you . . .

There's a hook to that. You're finding your rhythm. Hitting your own note. Striking your own chord.

Maybe your voice will crack as you try. Maybe you'll hit a wrong note. Or miss a verse. Maybe it will sound awful or funny or fantastic. Maybe it will be an entirely new type of music that changes things forever.

You won't know until you try. It's your song, and only you know how it goes.

So, don't worry if it's not perfect. It's not supposed to be. It's just supposed to be *real*. The real you.

By the way, did you ever notice that the people who claim

"I'm perfect" are as

Imperfect as the rest of us?

They're just less real. They make less impact. They have less courage. Their songs don't get remembered.

TIME TO RECAP:

YOU'VE GOT A SECRET POWER.

YOU MATTER.

YOU REJECT THE REJECTIONS.

YOU DON'T MAKE BAD DEALS.

YOU CHANGE THE CHANNEL.

YOU USE YOUR OWN VOICE.

YOU LIKE WHAT YOU LIKE.

YOU TEAM UP WITH PEOPLE LIKE YOU.

YOU CAN NEVER BE TOO MUCH OF YOU.

YOU GET—AND KEEP—PERSPECTIVE.

you are

PERFECTLY IMPERFECT

That's a lot of work right there—a lot of progress toward you. And you deserve a break.

Get your nose out of this book, and go do you. In whatever form. In whatever way. However feels right for you.

If you aren't quite sure of the whatever and however of you just yet, consider this:

There are nearly 40 *million* books for sale online besides this one.

So, you can be absolutely sure that the world is filled with other people who will be interesting to you or interested in you or curious about you.

And there are more ways than ever to find them and connect with them. So, even if your immediate circle or school situation isn't everything you want it to be yet, there are all kinds of communities to learn about online.

Just remember to apply all these same lessons there, too, as you explore and do you.

So, get to it. Get out there. And take note of what worked and what can work better.

We've got much more to do,

because there is much more to you.

PEOPLE WHO THINK THEY ARE PERFECT
LIKE TO HAVE OTHER PEOPLE
AROUND THEM TELLING THEM HOW
GREAT THEY ARE. BECAUSE INSIDE THEY
KNOW THEY ARE REALLY PHONIES.

—ERIC, ATLANTA

ON SOME OF MY DARKEST DAYS, THE
MUSIC IN MY MIND WOULD KEEP
MY HEAD UP HIGH AND MY EYES DRY.

—JOHN, UNITED KINGDOM

THE "DO" PLAN

What are you going to go do that will be an expression of what you are most curious about? What new interests are you going to explore? Who will join you, if anybody? Will you do you in an online community or IRL? Make some notes about what turned out well and what wasn't right for you (and why). These notes will help you find the right ways to build a good group of friends who share your interests.

I am curious about:

_____

_____

_____

I will explore these by doing:

_____

_____

_____

I am more comfortable in these communities:

_____

_____

_____

This worked:

_____

_____

_____

This sucked:

_____

_____

_____

So, what did you do, when you decided to go do you?

Find a new game? Make a new friend? Discover a new band? Invent a new sandwich?! Learn to read backwards? ?sdrawkcab daer ot nraeL

Honestly, it doesn't so much matter what you did, but that you did whatever was real for you. Each act of doing is a big step in becoming you.

Saying *yes* to whatever is right for you is saying *no* to the bullies.

Think how great life will be if you just keep on living like that—living like you. Rather than collapsing as the bullies want you to, you might just . . .

12
proof
POSITIVE

Graduate at the top of your class.

Go to your dream college.

Find a whole new group of friends.

Discover that amazing people love you for you.

Decide that quiet comfort is awesome.

Declare that loud rebellion is awesomer.

Get in shape.

Dance the night away.

Become crazy successful and

dominate the universe!

You just can't know the results until you do you. Whatever you decide to do, be true to yourself. Be the *proof positive* that your life is just right for you.

After all, who else is going to live it, if not you?

> " Comic books and fantasy fiction helped me on a daily basis. They represented a diverse group that didn't discriminate against people for their skin color, religion, or who they loved. "
>
> —JUSTIN, PENNSYLVANIA

BE
TRUE
TO YOURSELF.

#DOYOU

13

TOUGH
love

It should be pretty clear by now:

Getting through the tough moments isn't easy. But you don't need easy. You are stronger than you know. You decided to read this book, and you decided to *do* something to change things. Rather than just tolerating your pain or hiding your feelings, you took a deep breath. And decided to do you.

That's an act of love. For you, from you.

Because it's not easy to do that, especially when others are being unkind, let's recognize how important a step this is.

♡ DOING YOU IS LOVING YOU. ♡

Maybe that's a little corny-sounding. Maybe it isn't. But think about how many times you say, "I love that!" Well, that "that" . . . can be you. True story: It's fine to say, "I love pizza" or "I love unicorns." So, it should also be fine to say, "I love me." After all, you're *way* better than pizza and unicorns!

It's really that simple. Being true to you—everything that makes up you—is a real form of respect and protection. And it's pretty solid proof that the bullies aren't going to win. Not when you have love tougher than their hate.

You are strong enough to love you.

Bold enough to do you.

SO, READY FOR A REALITY Check?

Bullying is real, serious, damaging, and painful. It lasts—sometimes a lifetime.

But not every struggle is bullying.

Not every disagreement is bullying.

Not every moment of joking or teasing is bullying.

Bullying isn't about not getting what you want.

Bullying is about someone intimidating, ridiculing, and humiliating you. It's about someone preventing you from being you emotionally or physically.

Be tough enough to ask yourself, *Am I upset that I'm not getting my way? Or is someone purposefully trying to intimidate me and stop me from being me?* Bullying is powerful, and it's important to call it what it is—and what it isn't.

You might not
always get
what you want, but
you should always
be able to **do you**
no matter what
is happening
around you.

YOU ARE

STRONG ENOUGH

TO LOVE YOU

#DOYOU

This tough moment will serve you well. You may find that the bullying you are suffering is 100 percent real and must be dealt with. And you might also find that at least some of it is pain you can let go of. Unpleasant, maybe even unfair, but not bullying.

If that act of tough love reveals that you aren't dealing with a case of bullying, it means that you can get on with doing you, and not focus on the unpleasant things that would bother anybody.

Be strong enough and clear enough to take on the real bullies. And be strong enough and clear enough to let go of the stuff that just didn't go your way. There will be a next time.

You might not always get what you want, but you should always be able to do you no matter what is happening around you.

 My friends, my passion for learning, my dog … these all mattered more to me than the mean person who made me miserable.…
I loved my life outside of school, so I focused on those things.

—EVAN, VIRGINIA

Does all this talk of you mean that it's okay to be a selfish jerk and to think only of yourself and never anybody else?

This is a good question to ask, and asking it is an important step in the journey to you. We are going to keep asking tough questions. Your decision to do you means you get to be in control of both the questions and the answers now. And *that* is the opposite of living life under a bully.

Because you've been through some very painful things, you are probably more sensitive and aware than other people might be. So, let's agree that the strength to do you doesn't mean ignoring everyone else's needs or feelings. You aren't about to be a bully, after all.

In fact, part of your commitment to do you might include a commitment to do good things for other people, such as friends and family, or for causes that you believe in, such as animal welfare, the environment, and so on.

14

SELF-

centered

— *or* —

CENTERED

self?

The goal here is to do you so you find a centered self. Not so you become self-centered.

Doing you,

finding you,

being you.

With these as your focus, you can give yourself to the ideas, efforts you care about, and the people who care about you as much as you care about them.

That's what's called *love*. And it's the very opposite of bullying.

Yes, doing you is the healing act that is most required for a happy life.

And the best news? You are getting closer and closer to it with each page of this book.

> If I were ever to be cruel to someone else, then I would become like the aggressors from my past. If I have a strong heart and mind, then I should not need to bully anyone, ever.
>
> **—MATTHEW, UNITED KINGDOM**

DOING YOU, FINDING YOU, BEING YOU.

15

GIVE

AND

take

Most people would agree that the world is divided into givers and takers. Sad but true.

As you do you, you have important things to consider. What kind of you do you want to be?

When two takers get together . . . nothing much can happen. Things collapse into the emptiness.

When a giver and a taker get together . . . balance is hard to achieve. Things become one-sided quickly.

When two givers join forces . . . then something awesome can happen. Things grow and thrive and get better than before.

Bullies are takers. They've tried to take you from you. But you've taken yourself back, started down your own path, centered yourself, and asked some tough questions. You're ready for what's next. Namely, to share some of your talents. To give.

Doing you will become a courageous act of giving some of yourself to the world. It hasn't always been a kind place to you, and it might not be kind in the future. But the most rewarding part of doing you is giving of yourself where and when others will do the same.

As you give of yourself, remember that the most wonderful things to give are often intangible.

GIVE TIME.

GIVE IDEAS.

GIVE RESPECT.

GIVE COMPANY.

GIVE HELP.

GIVE THANKS.

Giving is one of the very best ways to do you.

As you give to what matters in your life, it will give
back to you. You will become surrounded by people
who care about you and give as generously as you do.

And, if the bullies gather again, you will have the
strength of a community of givers to turn to.

Give together.

Live together.

By doing you and giving you, the isolation that bullies
once created will collapse upon itself. *Bam!*

GIVING TO, NOT GIVING UP

How do you like to give? What do you want to share? Who needs your thoughts, time, understanding, or help? Make a list of all the things you can do, what you have to give, and all the places where you can share your talents.

_____

_____

_____

_____

_____

_____

_____

_____

(Good job. That was writing. Now you have to go out and do the giving. Get to it—and to YOU!)

> I was left out a lot, pushed aside, and treated badly. It made me resolve to be kind and to give extra time to anyone I ever saw who was rejected. I've made some fantastic friends simply by reaching out to others who were ignored because they, too, were quiet or awkward like me.
>
> —PAUL, FLORIDA

Nobody needs to tell you what it is like to be alone.

What the loneliness feels like. How long the hours of worry can last. Or the dread of one more day of fear. You've been there, and staying there is not an option.

You decided to do you. To stand up for yourself. To get on with your life.

But there may be others around you who are still in that lonely place. Still worrying. Still fearful. They don't yet know how to do what you have done. They can't yet stand up for themselves.

It is important to help them. It is one of the best things you can do. Share what you have been through. Tell your story. It will give them strength to find their story. Like you, they need to know there is something to *do*.

There may have been a time when you could not defend yourself or help yourself. Now, with all the work you have done and all the confidence you have, you can defend and help yourself *and* others.

16

STAND

up

SHARE

WHAT
YOU
HAVE

BEEN THROUGH.

Be a champion for someone else who you see on the edge. Stand up for him or her. Stand up with him or her. Stand up when the person isn't in the room.

When you stand up for others,

You stand up for yourself all over again.

> I was in line at a coffee bar, and two young men behind me were talking about how 'fags' deserve beating. I play rugby and am heavily tattooed … so when I turned around and said I was gay and they should choose their next words carefully, they were surprised to say the least.
>
> —STEVE, UNITED KINGDOM

> I once stood up for a kid who was being bullied on the Metro. I'll never know what impact I had …
> but I do know that I was not only standing up for him, but for the bullied kid in me.
>
> —WALTER, WASHINGTON, D.C.

17

FACE

THE

fear

None of us can know what life will bring. Surely a mix of good and bad, thrilling and disappointing, awaits us all. We don't know what or when, but being ready for "whatever, whenever" is required.

That's why being strong matters. Why doing you matters. You have to do you every day. Because when things turn suddenly, you'll be ready. You will know with confidence that fear, intimidation, bullying, anxiety, and shame will not win. You are *you*, after all, and look at all you've already handled, survived, done, and won!

It's often said that pain generates greatness: great achievement, great art, great music, and great discoveries. There are superstars in sports, music, movies, business, and medicine who have survived incredibly tough starts, such as being abused as children, being bullied, coming from broken homes, and surviving assaults. But they ended up doing more than just surviving. They triumphed—just as you can and will.

Did they succeed because they had something to prove?

Did they strengthen their characters in the face of challenges?

Did they use their pain to create bright futures that seemed impossible?

YES, YES, AND YES!

With all that you've seen and experienced, with all your commitment to do you,

just imagine what you can and will achieve.

Just imagine what a life full of you will be like.

Just imagine what's next when you do you.

> Has some good come out of being bullied? Hell yes! I am a far stronger person, and far more understanding. I believe we are a sum of our experiences, and we have two ways of interpreting what happens to us: becoming bitter and twisted, or learning from each painful event. I chose the latter.
>
> —GARY, OREGON

JUST
IMAGINE
WHAT'S
NEXT

WHEN YOU DO YOU.

#DOYOU

Oh, there it is. The voice of worry. The second-guessing. The echo of the bully in the hall. It can't be this easy. If it were, things wouldn't be so bad.

Sound about right?

This moment will happen many times over. You'll feel focused, prepared, and strong—and then it will all get challenged. An old fear will creep in. A moment of self-doubt. A reminder of what you went through. Bullying is very painful because it lasts so long—in many cases, it lasts long after the actual event. It can change you.

So, be ready for the moments that don't go so smoothly, okay?

Ask someone you trust to read the following questions aloud. It can be a family member, a teacher, or a friend. Or, if you prefer, you can read them out loud to yourself. After all, you trust you, too.

18

wait

JUST A

MINUTE

Bullying is
very painful because
it lasts so long—
in many cases, it
lasts long after the
actual event.
It can
change you.

DO YOU REALLY NEED THE PAIN TO STOP?

DO YOU WANT LIFE TO MOVE FORWARD?

DO YOU NEED MORE FUN?

DO YOU WANT REAL FRIENDS?

DO YOU BELIEVE YOU DESERVE HAPPINESS?

DO YOU TRUST YOUR OWN HEART?

DO YOU SEE WHAT'S POSSIBLE?

DO YOU DO WHAT'S RIGHT FOR YOU?

DO YOU KNOW THE BULLIES ARE WRONG?

DO YOU KNOW THAT YOU'RE OKAY JUST AS YOU ARE?

DO YOU ASK THE TOUGH QUESTIONS?

DO YOU ANSWER THEM HONESTLY?

DO YOU HAVE GOOD THINGS TO SHARE?

DO YOU STAND UP FOR OTHERS AND YOURSELF?

DO YOU GET SCARED SOMETIMES?

DO YOU KEEP PUSHING FORWARD?

DO YOU DO YOU?
YES, YOU DO.

19

DON'T

undo

Peer pressure. Popularity. Perfection.

Sometimes, bullying might not be personal. Or even intentional. It might come from a culture that says you aren't good enough.

It's as important to say no to these forces as it is to say no to the overt bullying or exclusion you may have already suffered. These cultural forces can make you feel just as lonely or unworthy. And they can be hard to resist because they don't come from a single source.

The unrealistic expectations of a group, the media, or pop-culture can erode your commitment to do you.

They can *undo* you.

You have fought hard to find you, so fight equally hard to keep you. Remind yourself of all the things that are right about you—and *do* those things! Any force that aims to make you feel bad, inadequate, excluded, or unwelcomed is something to be wary of. It can put you back in an emotional place that leaves you vulnerable.

> **"** The toughest part about bullying was that it changed how I thought about myself. The wounds in my mind remain, and even as an adult I can sometimes feel like I'm not worth being included. I remind myself in that exact moment that it is time to go live the life I've built for myself or the bullies can still win. **"**
>
> —TODD, MISSOURI

After the real bullies of everyday life are out of your life, be sure to keep clear of the bullying influences that can undo you and the work you have done to do you.

A commitment to do you isn't just for a moment. It's not just in a crisis. It's not about another person. It's a way of living. It's about being true to yourself—no matter how old you are or where you go.

ONCE YOU DO YOU

DON'T LET ANYTHING OR ANYONE UNDO YOU.

THE STAND UP INITIATIVE

The world isn't likely to get easier or nicer any time soon. To be ready for whatever, whenever, make a proactive plan for how to protect yourself and others. What five things do you most need to be ready for? What five fears do you need to address in advance? And what five friends do you need to reach out to and stand up with?

I need to be ready for:

1. _____
2. _____
3. _____
4. _____
5. _____

I need to address these fears:

1. _____
2. _____
3. _____
4. _____
5. _____

I can reach out to and stand up with these friends:

1. _____
2. _____
3. _____
4. _____
5. _____

Some encouragement, some tough love, some questions, and some planning.

That's all you needed to do you.

The answers, after all, are in you. They have been all along. And you have, hopefully, found some of them—the ones you need right now—by taking the time to read this book.

20

promise

YOURSELF

NOW IT'S TIME TO MAKE A PROMISE.

FROM YOU, *TO* YOU.

That you will never, ever sit quietly when you suffer.

That you will reach out when you hurt.

That you will believe in yourself, even if—especially if—others don't.

That you will get mad when you have to.

That you will let it all out.

That you will work to center yourself when you feel lost.

That you will take action when you feel stuck.

That you will reject the lies your doubts whisper to you.

That you will give what you can.

That you will help others.

That you will keep asking tough questions.

That you will embrace your fears.

That you will hold true to what makes you strong.

That you will love yourself with all your heart.

That you will never stop, no matter what, no matter why.

That you will *be*, even when you want to fade.

That you will do *you*.

PROMISE THAT. RIGHT HERE.
→ RIGHT NOW. ←

Why? Because
you are,
quite simply, the
best you there
will ever be.
And you deserve an
unbreakable
promise to you.

DO YOU

You've got a secret power.

You matter.

You reject the rejections.

You don't make bad deals.

You change the channel.

You use your own voice.

You like what you like.

You team up with people like you.

You can never be too much of you.

You get—and keep—perspective.

You are perfectly imperfect.

You are proof positive that you know what's best.

You love the stuff that makes you *you*.

You aren't afraid of the truth and can handle some tough love when it's deserved.

You have a centered self but are not self-centered.

You give more than you take.

You stand up for others and for yourself.

You face the fear.

You get ready for moments that don't go smoothly.

You won't let anything undo you.

You promise yourself.

You do you.

DO YOU